Berlin 24h

Verkehrskanzel Kurfürstendamm,
Ecke Joachimsthaler Straße

Traffic podium, Kurfürstendamm,
Corner of Joachimsthaler Strasse

Kurfürstendamm angolo
Joachimsthaler Strasse,
postazione sopraelevata per
la regolazione del traffico

クアフュルステンダム通り
とヨアヒムスターラーシュ
トラーセ通りとの交 差点に
ある交通整理の台

nicolai

Erik-Jan Ouwerkerk

deutsch   english
italiano   日本語

Berlin 24h

Vorwort

Spätestens seit der Vereinigung übt Berlin eine anscheinend unwiderstehliche Anziehungskraft aus. Warum wollen, warum kommen alle nach Berlin? Die Stadt hat nicht die Schönheit zu bieten, mit der Paris begeistert, nicht die Unüberschaubarkeit, die an London reizt, nicht die Internationalität, die New York ausstrahlt. Was Berlin so verlockend macht, ist das Leben, das sich in dieser Stadt, die viel jünger ist als andere Metropolen und im 20. Jahrhundert gleich mehrfach Zerstörung und Selbstzerstörung erlebt hat, immer wieder einnistet und behauptet. Berlin lebt – und das 24 Stunden jeden Tag.

Seit 1949 kennt Berlin keine Sperrstunde. Dieser Umstand ist das Ergebnis eines kuriosen Wettrüstens, das auf einem der vielen Randschauplätze des Kalten Krieges stattfand: Ost- und Westsektoren überboten sich eine Zeit lang wechselseitig mit dem stetigen Hinausschieben der Sperrstunde – bis die Kommandanten der Westsektoren schließlich auf Initiative des Obermeisters der Gaststätten-Innung Heinz Zellermayer am 20. Juni 1949 mit einem Schlag den Wettstreit siegreich beendeten und die Sperrstunde ganz aufhoben. Seitdem hat Berlin zumindest fürs Tanzen, Feiern und Trinken tatsächlich 24 Stunden geöffnet.

Aber auch sonst kommt die Stadt nicht zur Ruhe, und sie will es auch gar nicht. Wenn die Ersten frühmorgens zur Arbeit gehen, sind die Letzten vom Vorabend noch lange nicht auf dem Weg nach Hause. Während es in vielen Nachtclubs erst richtig losgeht, werden auf den Großmärkten bereits die frischen Waren für den Tag verteilt. Und während die Touristen sich gegenseitig vor dem Brandenburger Tor fotografieren, schlafen sich die Nachtschwärmer für den nächsten Ausflug aus. Wenn es an einem Ort still wird, braust an einem anderen das Leben auf. Berlin ist immer eine Stadt des Tempos gewesen – und eine Stadt der Gleichzeitigkeit, in der an den unterschiedlichsten Orten etwas passiert. Wie viel man auch sieht, erlebt und kennen lernt – man hat immer das meiste verpasst.

Alles hat in Berlin seine Zeit oder seine Zeiten, und umgekehrt kann Berlin nur erfassen, wer sich auf alle Facetten einlässt und eine Reise durch die vielen Welten eines kompletten Berliner Tages unternimmt. Die Dynamik dieser Stadt hat verschiedene Rhythmen, die sich gegenseitig überlagern, die kein einheitliches und schon gar kein eingängiges Bild Berlins zulassen. Wer beispielsweise nur die Serie der Sehenswürdigkeiten in Erinnerung behält, hat sicherlich ein falsches Bild. Denn selbst die werden von den Berlinern und Berlin-Besuchern zu verschiedenen Tages- und Nachtzeiten mitunter zu ganz unterschiedlichen Aktivitäten genutzt, sie verändern nicht nur ihre Erscheinung, sondern auch ihre Funktion und ihre Bedeutung.

Die Dynamik, das Nebeneinander und das Ungleichzeitige, nicht die Architektur oder das Stadtbild ist der Zusammenhang Berlins. Deswegen setzt sich das Bild dieser Stadt immer wieder neu zusammen – rund um die Uhr, bis zum Anfang eines neuen Tags.

Preface

Berlin has exerted a seemingly irresistible power of attraction, certainly since reunification. What brings so many here? Why do they want to come? The city doesn't have the beauty that excites admiration in Paris. Nor does it have the vastness that is London's charm or the international atmosphere of New York. The secret to Berlin's seductiveness is its vitality. In a city so much younger than other metropoli, one that experienced repeated destruction and self-destruction in the twentieth century, new life always finds its place and continually asserts itself. Berlin lives – 24 hours a day.

Berlin's bars and restaurants haven't known a "last call" since 1949. This state of affairs is the result of a curious sort of arms race that took place in one of the Cold War's many minor theatres; the eastern and western sectors sought for some time to outbid one another by continually extending closing times. Finally, on June 20, 1949, the commanding officer of the western sector won the contest in one blow by completely lifting the licensing law. (This was on the initiative of Heinz Zellermayer, then head of the restaurateur's guild.) Since then, Berlin has in fact been open 24-hours-a-day – for dancing, drinking, and having fun.

But the city doesn't sleep in other ways either. It doesn't want to. In the early morning, as the first people are heading off to work, the last from the night before are still a long way from home. Just as things are heating up in the city's many night clubs, fresh products for the new day are already being laid out in the wholesale markets. And while the tourists are photographing each other in front of the Brandenburg Gate, the night crawlers are sleeping it off and resting up for their next outing. No sooner have things calmed down in one place then new life erupts somewhere else. Berlin has always been a briskly paced city, a city of simultaneity. Something is always happening in the most diverse settings. No matter how much of the city you've met, seen, and experienced – you've still missed most of it.

Everything in Berlin has its time – or times. Inversely, the only way to grasp Berlin is to engage all of its facets, to undertake a journey through the many worlds of a full Berlin day. This city's dynamic has many rhythms. They overlay each other without yielding a uniform picture – certainly not one that can be absorbed easily. Anyone, for example, who leaves town with just the memory of a series of landmarks definitely has the wrong picture. For, depending on the time of day or night, even these are used for different activities by Berliners and Berlin's visitors, changing not only their appearance but also their function and their meaning.

Berlin's identity doesn't consist of its architecture or its views but of its dynamic, its adjacency and simultaneity. The city thus perpetually remakes itself – around the clock. Until a new day begins.

Prefazione

Al più tardi a partire dalla riunificazione pare che il fascino di Berlino sia divenuto irresistibile. Perché tutti vogliono venire a Berlino? Perché tutti ci vengono? Non offre l'appariscente bellezza che entusiasma chi visita Parigi. Non è disorientante, e quindi intrigante, come Londra. Non emana lo charme cosmopolita di New York. A rendere Berlino così seducente è la vita che si cela in ogni anfratto di questa metropoli molto più giovane di altre capitali, che nel ventesimo secolo ha subìto e superato varie distruzioni e autodistruzioni. Una vita che si autoafferma giorno dopo giorno. Berlino è una città che vive senza sosta 24 ore al giorno.

Dal 1949 Berlino non conosce orari di chiusura dei locali. Una circostanza dovuta ad una bizzarra corsa agli armamenti disputata su uno dei numerosi palcoscenici secondari della Guerra Fredda. Per un certo periodo i settori est ed ovest della città fecero a gara a chi posticipava di più l'ora di chiusura dei locali, finché il 20 giugno del 1949, su iniziativa del presidente dell'Associazione degli esercenti, Heinz Zellermayer, i comandanti dei settori occidentali decisero di concludere e vincere la competizione con un colpo di mano, abolendo del tutto l'ora di chiusura. Da allora Berlino è una città effettivamente aperta 24 ore su 24, per lo meno quando si tratta di ballare, bere e festeggiare.

Ma anche in generale è una città che non si ferma mai. E nemmeno vuole farlo. La mattina presto, quando i primi Berlinesi si recano al lavoro, gli ultimi ancora svegli dalla sera precedente sono ben lungi dall'avviarsi verso casa. Mentre nei numerosi locali notturni l'atmosfera comincia a riscaldarsi, ai mercati generali inizia la distribuzione della merce fresca. E mentre i turisti si fanno immortalare davanti alla Porta di Brandeburgo, i nottambuli dormono il sonno ristoratore che gli permetterà di affrontare il prossimo giro notturno. Quando in un punto della città scende il silenzio, in un altro si risveglia la vita. Berlino è sempre stata una città costantemente in corsia di sorpasso, una città delle concomitanze, dove le cose accadono contemporaneamente nei luoghi più disparati. Per quanto si veda, si viva e si conosca, la maggior parte delle cose sfugge ugualmente.

A Berlino ogni cosa ha un suo tempo o suoi tempi. Viceversa, solo chi si adegua alle diverse sfaccettature di Berlino e intraprende un viaggio attraverso gli innumerevoli mondi che compongono una giornata berlinese, potrà capirla a fondo. Berlino si muove seguendo ritmi diversi, ritmi che si sovrappongono l'uno all'altro, che non permettono di farsene un quadro unitario e tanto meno univoco. Coloro a cui, ad esempio, restano impressi nella memoria solo i monumenti e le bellezze artistiche, avranno sicuramente un'immagine sbagliata della città, perché anche quelli vengono usati dai Berlinesi e dai visitatori ad ogni ora del giorno e della notte per attività di diversissima natura che ne mutano non solo l'aspetto, ma anche la funzione ed il significato.

Sono la dinamica, le vite parallele e le sfasature temporali, non l'architettura o il paesaggio urbanistico, a creare la trama di Berlino. Per questo l'immagine della città è in continuo mutamento, 24 ore su 24, giorno dopo giorno.

はじめに

統合後のベルリンはどうしようもなく人を惹きつけてやまないらしい。
何故全てがベルリンに集中するのか、どうして皆ベルリンに来てしまう
のでしょう?パリの様に人を夢中にさせる美しさも、ロンドンの様な見
通しのきかない面白さも、ニューヨークの世界性もない町なのに。その
魅力は、他のメトロポールよりずっと若く、20世紀に幾度もの破壊と
自己破壊の経験を持つこの都市に繰り返し根づき主張する生命力な
のです。ベルリンは生きています－それも毎日、24時間。

1949年以来ベルリンには法定閉店時刻がありません。これは、冷戦
時代いくつもあった、奇妙な東西競争の所産のひとつなのです。東西
に分かれていたベルリンが閉店時刻を競って遅らせ合った時期があり
ました。それが当時飲食店団体の長であったハインツ・ツェラーマイヤ
ーの貢献によって、西ベルリン側の司令官が1949年6月20日につい

に競争に終止符を打ち、法定閉店時刻をなくしてしまったのです。それ以来ベルリンはダンスやパーティーや飲食に関しては24時間オープンなのです。

そうでなくてもこの町は静まることを知りません、静まろうともしません。早朝一番に職場へ急ぐ人がいると思えば、前夜を楽しんだ人たちはまだ家路についていません。たくさんのナイトクラブが盛りの頃、大きな市場ではその日の新鮮な食品の搬入、仕分けを行っています。観光客がブランデンブルガートーア門の前でポーズをとっている間、夜型人間たちは次のパーティーのために寝だめをし、静まる所があれば活気に溢れる所がある。ベルリンはいつもテンポの速い町 – そして様々な場所でいつも何かが起こっている町。どんなにたくさんのものを見ても、経験しても、結局大抵のものを逃してしまう、そんな町なのです。

ベルリンではあらゆることが独自の時間で動いている、逆にベルリンはその全ての場面を受け入れられる人、または、そのたくさんの世界を旅することのできる人でなければ把握できる都市ではありません。その活気の元はそれぞれ重なり合う様々なリズムで、一様な、もっと言えばただ単純なベルリン像などはないと言っていいでしょう。一連の名所だけを頭に入れる人があるとしたら、それでは間違ったベルリン像を作ってしまう。即ちベルリンっ子とそこを訪れる人たちは昼と夜の時間帯によってまったく違ったイベントに使い、その外観だけでなく、機能や意味合いさえも変えてしまうのです。

ベルリンを作っているのは建築でも都市像でもなく、ダイナミックに平行して、しかも同時に起こっていない全ての事柄なのです。そうしてこの町の像は始終新しく組み合わされているのです – 四六時中、また新しい日が始まるまで。

00:00 - 24:00

00:00

Lustgarten vor dem Alten Museum

The Lustgarten, in front of the
Altes Museum

Lustgarten davanti all'Altes Museum

アルテス ムゼウム美術館前
のルストガルテン庭園

00:15

Im Nachtclub »Adagio«,
Marlene-Dietrich-Platz

In the Adagio nightclub
on Marlene Dietrich Platz

Nel night club « Adagio »,
Marlene-Dietrich-Platz

マルレーネ・ディートリ
ッヒ・プラッツ広場のナ
イトクラブ "アダージョ"

00:30

BVG-Haus am Landwehrkanal,
links ein »Rosinenbomber« am
Deutschen Technik Museum

The BVG office building (housing the
city's public transport company) on
the Landwehr Canal. At left, suspended
in front of the German Museum of
Technology, is a so-called "raisin-
bomber" used during the Berlin Airlift

Centro direzionale della BVG lungo
il Landwehrkanal, a sinistra, davanti
al Museo della Tecnica, un cosiddetto
«Rosinenbomber», i bombardieri usati
per il ponte aereo

ラントヴェアカナル運河沿いの
BVG ハウス、左にドイツ技術博
物館の "ロジ ーネンボンバー"

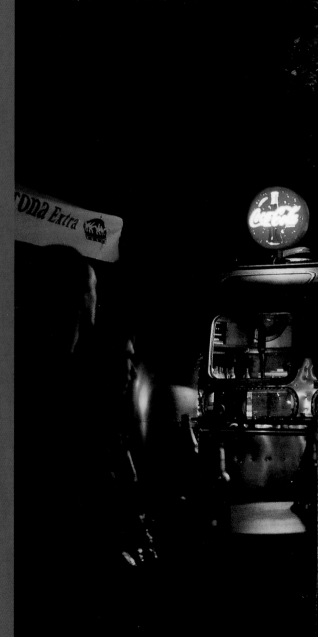

00:45

Columbia Diner, Columbiadamm

Columbia Diner, Columbiadamm

Columbia Diner, Columbiadamm

コロンビアダムにあるコロ
ンビア・ダイナー

01:00

Zeitungsdruckerei in Lichtenberg

Newspaper printer, Lichtenberg

Tipografia a Lichtenberg

リヒテンベルク新聞印刷所

01:15

Weltzeituhr am Alexanderplatz

The "world clock" on Alexanderplatz

Orologio universale ad Alexanderplatz

アレクサンダープラッツ広場の
世界時間時計

KREUZBERG

01:30

Bergmannstraße, Kreuzberg

Bergmannstrasse, Kreuzberg

Bergmannstrasse, quartiere di Kreuzberg

ベルクマンシュトラーセ通り、
クロイツベルク地区

01:45

Party im ehemaligen Postbahnhof

Party in the former Postbahnhof
(Postal Station)

Party nell'ex Stazione di Posta

かつてのポストバーンホ
フ駅でのパーティー

02:00

Haifischbar, Kreuzberg

Haifisch bar, Kreuzberg

Haifischbar, quartiere di Kreuzberg

ハイフィッシュバー、
クロイツベルク地区

02:15

Betonierarbeiten nahe
des Anhalter Bahnhofs

Concrete works near
Anhalter Station

Lavori di getto nei
pressi dell'ex stazione
di Anhalter Bahnhof

アンハルター・バ
ーンホフ駅近くの
コンクリ打ち

02:30

Yorckstraße, Ecke Groß-
beerenstraße, Kreuzberg

The corner of Yorckstrasse
and Großbeerenstrasse,
Kreuzberg

Yorckstrasse angolo
Grossbeerenstrasse,
quartiere di Kreuzberg

ヨルクシュトラーセ
通りとグロースベー
レンシュトラーセ通
りとの交差点

02:45

Ehemalige Staatsbank in der Französischen Straße,
Vorführung von Filmen aus dem Staatsbankarchiv
rund um die Uhr

The former Staatsbank on Französische Strasse,
which shows films from the Staatsbank archive
around the clock

Ex Banca di Stato nella Französische Strasse,
proiezione 24 ore su 24 di film dell'archivio della
Banca di Stato

フランツォージッシェシュトラーセ通
りの旧国立銀行、国立銀行保管の映画が
一日中上映されている

03:00

Tankstelle,
Chausseestraße

A gas station,
Chausseestrasse

Stazione di rifornimento,
Chausseestrasse

ショセーシュト
ラーセ通りのガソ
リンスタンド

03:15

Sage Club,
Köpenicker Straße

Sage Club,
Köpenicker Strasse

Discoteca Sage Club,
Köpenicker Strasse

ザーゲ・クラブ、
キョペニッカーシ
ュトラーセ通り

03:30

In der Stresemannstraße, Kreuzberg

On Stresemannstrasse, Kreuzberg

Nella Stresemannstrasse, quartiere di Kreuzberg

シュトレーゼマンシュトラーセ通り、
クロイツベルク地区

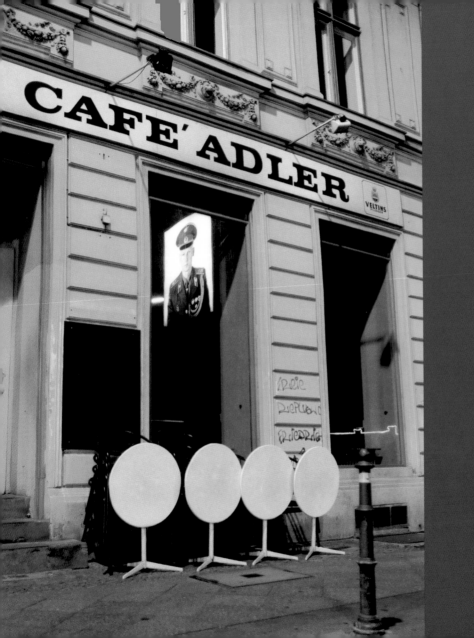

03:45

Café Adler am Checkpoint Charlie

Café Adler at Checkpoint Charlie

Caffè Adler a Checkpoint Charlie

チェックポイント・チャーリーのカフェ アードラー

04:00

Fruchthof, Gemüsegroßmarkt
Beusselstraße

The fruit court of the wholesale
vegetable market, Beusselstrasse

Mercato della frutta nei magazzini
ortofrutticoli della Beusselstrasse

ボイセルシュトラーセ通りの
野菜市場にある果物屋

04:15

Party in einem Club in der
Straße der Pariser Kommune

Party in a Club on the
Strasse der Pariser Kommune

Party in un club nella
Strasse der Pariser Kommune

パリーザー コンミュー
ンの通りにあるクラブの
パーティー風景

Staatsoper und Humboldt-Universität,
Unter den Linden

The Staatsoper and Humboldt University,
Unter den Linden

Edificio dell'Opera e Humboldt-Universität,
Unter den Linden

国立オペラ座とフンボルト大学、
ウンター・デン・リンデン通り

Siegessäule, Tiergarten

Siegessäule (the victory column), Tiergarten

La Colonna della Vittoria, quartiere di Tiergarten

ティアガルテン地区の
ジーゲスゾイレ柱

05:00

Teilrekonstruktion der Bauakademie
und Friedrichwerdersche Kirche,
Am Werderschen Markt

A reconstructed portion of the
Bauakademie and the Friedrich-
werdersche Church,
Am Werderschen Markt

Parziale ricostruzione della facciata
dell'ex Accademia di Architettura
e Friedrichwerdersche Kirche,
Am Werderschen Markt

一部復元されている建築大学と
フリードリヒヴェルダーの教会、
ヴェルダーシャマルクト広場

STILLE

05:15

Parkhaus im Stilwerk, Kantstraße

The parking garage at the Stilwerk
design centre, Kantstrasse

Autorimessa nel grande magazzino
del design Stilwerk, Kantstrasse

シュティールヴェルク内の駐車場、
カントシュトラーセ通り

05:30

U-Bahnhof Stadtmitte

Stadtmitte U-Bahn station

Stazione della metropolitana
di Stadtmitte

地下鉄駅シュタットミッテ

05:45

Bäckerei in Prenzlauer Berg

A bakery in Prenzlauer Berg

Panificio nel quartiere
di Prenzlauer Berg

プレンツラウアーベルク
地区のパン屋

06:00

S-Bahnhof Ostkreuz,
Zug nach Pankow

Ostkreuz S-Bahn station,
a Pankow-bound train

Stazione di Ostkreuz, treno
urbano in direzione Pankow

S-バーン駅オストクロイ
ツ、パンコフ行きの電車

06:15

Blumengroßmarkt,
Friedrichstraße

The wholesale flower market,
Friedrichstrasse

Mercato dei fiori,
Friedrichstrasse

花市、フリードリヒシュ
トラーセ通り

 06:30

Mehringhof, Kreuzberg

Mehringhof, Kreuzberg

Mehringhof, quartiere di Kreuzberg

メーリングホーフ、
クロイツベルク地区

06:45

S-Bahnhof Ostkreuz

Ostkreuz S-Bahn station

Stazione di Ostkreuz

S-バーン駅オストクロイツ

07:00

Im Tiergarten

In the Tiergarten

Nel parco di Tiergarten

ティアガルテン地区

07:15

Busbahnhof Steglitz

The Steglitz bus station

Terminale degli autobus di Steglitz

バスの駅シュテーグリッツ

07:30

Im Tiergarten

In the Tiergarten

Nel parco di Tiergarten

ティアガルテン地区

07:45

Am Potsdamer Platz

On Potsdamer Platz

Potsdamer Platz

ポツダム広場

08:00

Kreuzbergstraße,
Ecke Großbeerenstraße, Kreuzberg

The corner of Kreuzbergstrasse
and Großbeerenstrasse, Kreuzberg

Kreuzbergstrasse
angolo Grossbeerenstrasse,
quartiere di Kreuzberg

クロイツベルクシュトラー
セ通りとグロースベーレン
シュトラーセ通りとの交
差点、クロイツベルク地区

08:15

Deutscher Dom,
Gendarmenmarkt

The Deutscher Dom
on Gendarmenmarkt

Deutscher Dom,
Gendarmenmarkt

ドイチャー・ドー
ム教会、ジャンダル
メンマルクト広場

08:30

Fensterputzer im Sony Center

A window washer in the Sony Center

Lavavetri al Sony Center

ソニーセンターの窓拭き

08:45

Mauergedenkstätte Bernauer Straße

Bernauer Strasse Memorial to the
Berlin Wall

Centro di documentazione e sito com-
memorativo per le vittime del Muro
nella Bernauer Strasse

ベルナウアーシュトラーセ通り
りにあるベルリンの壁記念碑

09:00

Büro am Ostbahnhof

An office near the Ostbahnhof station

Uffici nei pressi della stazione
ferroviaria di Ostbahnhof

オストバーンホーフ駅のオ
フィス街

09:15

Schloss Bellevue,
Tiergarten

Bellevue Palace,
Tiergarten

Castello di Bellevue,
quartiere di Tiergarten

シュロス・ベルヴュ
ー城、ティアガルテ
ン地区

09:30

Der Regierende Bürgermeister
Klaus Wowereit am Brandenburger Tor

Governing Mayor Klaus Wowereit
at the Brandenburg Gate

Il Borgomastro di Berlino,
Klaus Wowereit, davanti alla
Porta di Brandeburgo

現市長クラウス・ヴォーヴェラ
イト、ブランデンブルク門にて

09:45

Öffnung des Tores am Haupteingang des KaDeWe

Doors open at the main entrance of the KaDeWe department store

Apertura dell'ingresso principale dei grandi magazzini KaDeWe

カーデーヴェーデパートの正面玄関が開く

10:00

Plenarsitzung im Deutschen Bundestag

Plenary session in the Bundestag
(German Federal Parliament)

Seduta plenaria del Parlamento Tedesco

ドイツ連邦議会の本会議

10:15

Quartier 205,
Friedrichstraße

Quartier 205,
Friedrichstrasse

Galleria commerciale
Quartier 205,
Friedrichstrasse

フリードリヒシュト
ラーセ通り 205 番地

10:30

Paul-Löbe-Haus,
Domizil der Bundestags-
abgeordneten
Konrad-Adenauer-Straße

Paul Löbe Building,
an office block for the members
of the German Parliament
Konrad Adenauer Strasse

Paul-Löbe-Haus,
sede degli uffici
dei parlamentari,
Konrad-Adenauer-Strasse

パウル・リョーベ・
ハウス、コンラッド
・アデナウアー・シュ
トラーセ通り

10:45

Fütterung der Eisbären im Zoo

Feeding the Polar Bears at the Zoo

Il pasto degli orsi polari allo zoo

動物園の白熊が餌を貰う

11:00

Zugang zur Messe während
der Funkausstellung

Entrance to Berlin's exhibition
and fair centre during the
broadcaster's fair

Verso il Palazzo delle Esposizioni
durante la Fiera Internazionale
dell'elettronica

フンクメッセ開催中のメ
ッセ入り口

11:15

Shaolin-Mönche vor dem
Brandenburger Tor

Shaolin monks in front
of the Brandenburg Gate

Monaci Shaolin davanti
alla Porta di Brandeburgo

ブランデンブルク門前
の少林寺僧

11:30

Fensterputzer
am Bahnhof Potsdamer Platz

A window washer
at the Potsdamer Platz Station

Lavavetri
alla stazione di Potsdamer Platz

ポツダーマープラッツ
駅の窓拭き

11:45

Am Alexanderplatz

On Alexanderplatz

Ad Alexanderplatz

アレクサンダープラッツ広場

12:00

Plenarsitzung im Deutschen Bundestag

Plenary session in the Bundestag
(German Federal Parliament)

Seduta plenaria del Parlamento Tedesco

ドイツ連邦議会の本会議

12:15

Vor dem Reichstagsgebäude

In front of the Reichstag

Davanti all'edificio del Reichstag

帝国議会議事堂前

12:30

Treppe des Schauspielhauses
am Gendarmenmarkt

The stairs of the Schauspielhaus
on Gendarmenmarkt

Scalinata della Schauspielhaus
a Gendarmenmarkt

ジャンダルメンマルク
ト広場にある劇場の階段

12:45

Berlin-Marathon
vor dem Roten Rathaus

The Berlin Marathon
in front of city hall – the "Rotes Rathaus"

La maratona di Berlino
passa davanti al Municipio Rosso

赤い市役所前のベルリン
・マラソン

13:00

Am Gleisdreieck

Gleisdreieck

A Gleisdreieck

グライスドライエック周辺

13:15

An der Oberbaumbrücke

On the Oberbaum Bridge

Vista sull'Oberbaumbrücke
dalla riva della Sprea

オーバーバウムブリュッケ橋

13:30

Lustgarten vor dem Alten Museum

The Lustgarten, in front of the Altes Museum

Lustgarten davanti all'Altes Museum

アルテス ムゼウム美術館前
のルストガルテン庭園

13:45

Zuschauertribüne
an der Galopprennbahn Hoppegarten

The spectator stands
at the Hoppegarten racetrack

Tribuna spettatori
nell'ippodromo di Hoppegarten

ホッペガルテン、
競馬場の観客席

14:00

Beach-Volleyball Grand Slam
am Schlossplatz

Beach-Volleyball Grand Slam
on Schlossplatz

Torneo di Beach Volley
nella Schlossplatz

シュロスプラッツ広場の
ビーチバレーボール、
グランド・スラム

14:15

Im Bus 119 unter den Yorckbrücken

On Bus 119 beneath the Yorck bridges

A bordo dell'autobus 119
sotto i ponti nella Yorckstrasse

ヨルクブリュッケ橋下を 119
番のバスで通る

14:30

Schiffsanlegestelle
am Berliner Dom

Ship moorings
in front of the Berliner Dom

Posto di attracco
davanti al Berliner Dom

ベルリーナードーム
寺院傍の船着き場

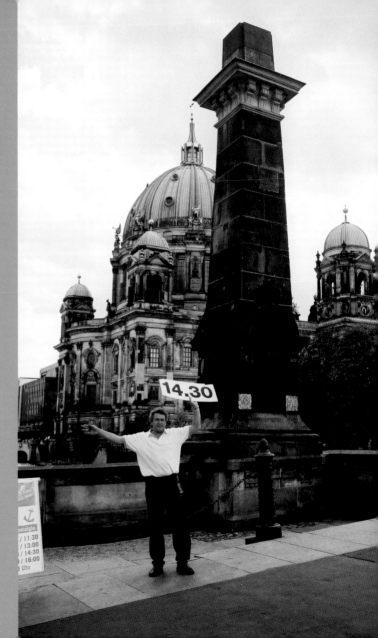

14:45

E.-T.-A.-Hoffmann-Garten,
Jüdisches Museum

E. T. A. Hoffmann Garden,
Jewish Museum

Il giardino di E.T.A. Hoffmann
nel Museo Ebraico

E.-T.-A.ホフマンガルテ
ン庭園、ユダヤ博物館

15:00

Im Quartier 206, Friedrichstraße

In the Quartier 206 shopping centre,
Friedrichstrasse

Nella galleria commerciale Quartier 206,
Friedrichstrasse

フリードリヒシュトラー
セ通り 206 番地

15:15

Flughafen Tegel

Tegel Airport

Aeroporto di Tegel

ベルリン、テーゲル空港

15:30

Hinterhof in Kreuzberg

A back courtyard
in Kreuzberg

Cortile interno
nel quartiere di Kreuzberg

クロイツベルク地
区にある中庭

15:45

East Side Gallery

The East Side Gallery

East Side Gallery

イーストサイド・
ギャラリー

16:00

Straßenumzug zum Christopher Street Day
am Potsdamer Platz

Street parade for Christopher Street Day
on Potsdamer Platz

Corteo lungo la Potsdamer Platz
in occasione del Christopher Street Day

ポツダム広場のＣＳＤ行列

16:15

Newton Bar, Charlottenstraße

Newton Bar, Charlottenstrasse

Newton Bar, Charlottenstrasse

シャルロッテンシュトラーセ
通りにあるニュートン・バー

16:30

Hertha-BSC-Fans im Olympia Stadion

Fans of the Hertha BSC football team
in the Olympia Stadium

Tifosi della squadra di calcio
Hertha BSC nello Stadio Olimpico

ヘルタ BSC サッカーチームの
ファン達、オリンピックスタ
ジアムで

16:45

Im Tiergarten

In the Tiergarten

Nel parco di Tiergarten

ティアガルテン地区

17:00

Im Glienicker Park

Glienicker Park

Nel Parco di Glienicke

グリーニッカーパルク公園

17:15

Bahnhof Zoo

Zoo Station

Stazione di Bahnhof Zoo

ツォーローギッシャ
ーガルテン駅

17:30

Im Garten der Liebermann-Villa
am Wannsee

The Liebermann Villa garden
on the Wannsee

Nel giardino di Villa Liebermann
a Wannsee

ヴァンゼー湖に面するリー
バーマン・ヴィラの庭園

17:45

Aufbau einer Ausstellung
von Hedi Slimane in der Galerie
»Kunst-Werke«, Mitte

A Hedi Slimane exhibition
being installed in the
Kunst Werke Gallery, Mitte

Allestimento di una mostra
di Hedi Slimane nella galleria
« Kunst-Werke », quartiere di Mitte

ギャラリー「クンスト・ヴェ
ルケ」でのヘーディ・スリマ
ネ展準備風景、ミッテ中央区

18:00

Kurfürstendamm

The Kurfürstendamm

Kurfürstendamm

クアフュルステンダム通り

18:15

Am Engelbecken in Kreuzberg

At the Engelbecken (angel basin)
in Kreuzberg

Passeggiata lungo l'Engelbecken,
quartiere di Kreuzberg

クロイツベルク地区にある
エンゲルベッケン

18:30

Im Liquidrom, Möckernstraße

In the Liquidrom, Möckernstrasse

Nel Liquidrom, Möckernstrasse

リクイドローム、
ミョンカーシュトラーセ通り

18:45

Oranienburger Straße, Mitte

Oranienburger Strasse, Mitte

Oranienburger Strasse, quartiere di Mitte

オラーニエンブルガーシュトラー
セ通り、ミッテ中央区

19:00

Empfang in den Kolonnaden
vor der Alten Nationalgalerie

A reception in the colonnade
in front of the Alte Nationalgalerie

Rinfresco sotto il colonnato
della Alte Nationalgalerie

アルテ・ナツィオナルガラ
リー美術館前、コロナーデン
でのレセプション

19:15

Humboldt-Universität und Zeughaus,
Unter den Linden

Humboldt University and the Zeughaus
(the old armory), Unter den Linden

Humboldt-Universität e Arsenale,
Unter den Linden

フンボルト大学とツォイクハウス、
ウンターデンリンデン通り

19:30

Vor dem Bundeskanzleramt

In front of the Bundeskanzleramt
(Federal chancellery)

Davanti alla Cancelleria Federale

連邦首相官房前

19:45

Blick von der Elsenbrücke
auf den »Molecule Man«
und die Oberbaumbrücke

A view from the Elsen Bridge
onto "Molecule Man" and the
Oberbaum Bridge

Vista sul « Molecule Man »
e sull'Oberbaumbrücke
dall'Elsenbrücke

エルゼンブリュッケ橋より
「モレキュール・マン」
とオーバーバウムブリュッ
ケ橋を望む

20:00

Am Hackeschen Markt

At Hackescher Markt

Hackescher Markt

ハッケッシャー
マルクト市場

20:15

»Bundespressestrand«
am Schiffbauerdamm

The "Bundespressestrand"
(Federal Press Beach)
stretching along the
Schiffbauerdamm

«Lido» davanti alla sede
dell'Ufficio Stampa del
Governo Federale sulla
Schiffbauerdamm

国際プレスセンター
前の岸辺「ブンデスプ
レッセシュトラント」、
シッフバウ アーダム

20:30

Freiluftkino vor der
Alten Nationalgalerie

The open air cinema in front
of the Alte Nationalgalerie

Cinema all'aperto davanti
alla Alte Nationalgalerie

アルテ・ナツィオナル
ガラリー美術館前のオ
ープンエア映画館

20:45

Großleinwand vor der Alten
Nationalgalerie mit Bildern
von der Maueröffnung
aus dem Film »Good bye, Lenin!«

Shots of the fall of the Berlin Wall
from the film "Good bye, Lenin!"
on the giant screen in front of the
Alte Nationalgalerie

Immagini della caduta del Muro tratte
dal film « Good bye, Lenin! » e proiettate
su uno schermo gigante nel cortile
della Alte Nationalgalerie

アルテ・ナツィオナルガラリー
美術館前の映画スクリーン、
上映中の「グッバ イ、レーニン」
ベルリンの壁崩壊シーン

21:00

Am Brandenburger Tor

At the Brandenburg Gate

Davanti alla Porta di Brandeburgo

ブランデンブルガー トーア門

21:15

Abgeordnetenbüro
im Paul-Löbe-Haus

An MP's office
in the Paul Löbe Building

Ufficio di un parlamentare
nella Paul-Löbe-Haus

パウル・リョーベ・ハウ
ス内にある議員オフィス

21:30

Skater auf dem Kurfürstendamm

In-line skater on Kurfürstendamm

Skater lungo la Kurfürstendamm

クアフュルステンダム通り
を行くスケーター

21:45

Filmpalast am Kurfürstendamm

The Filmpalast on Kurfürstendamm

Filmpalast sulla Kurfürstendamm

クアフュルステンダム通りの
フィルムパラスト映画館

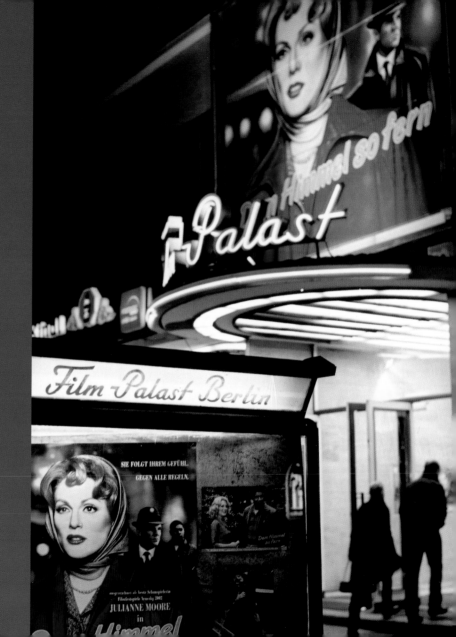

22:00

Zeitgenössische Oper im
Hebbel-Theater, Kreuzberg

Contemporary opera in the
Hebbel Theatre, Kreuzberg

Opera lirica moderna all'Hebbel
Theater, quartiere di Kreuzberg

ヘッベル・テアター劇場で
の現代オペラ上演、クロイ
ツベルク地区

22:15

Am Kulturforum

The Kulturforum

Kulturforum

クルトゥアフォー
ルム文化センター

22:30

Nach dem Konzert
in der Philharmonie

After a concert
at the Berlin Philharmonic

Dopo un concerto
alla Philharmonie

フィルハーモニーホー
ルでのコンサートの後

22:45

Feuerkünstler
am Hackeschen Markt

A street performer
at Hackescher Markt

Sputafuoco sul piazzale
di Hackescher Markt

ハッケッシャーマルク
ト市場の大道芸人

23:00

Sechstagerennen in der
Berlin Arena (Velodrom)

A six-day bicycle race at the
Berlin Arena (Velodrom)

La Sei giorni di ciclismo nel
velodromo della Berlin Arena

ベルリン アレナ競技場での
6 日間二輪競技（ヴェロド
ローム）

23:15

»Volxgolf« in der Chausseestraße

Volxgolf on Chausseestrasse

« Golf popolare » nella Chausseestrasse

ショセーシュトラーセ通りの
「フォルクスゴルフ」

23:30

Vertical Dance Performance
an einem Plattenbau in
Friedrichshain

Vertical dance performance
on a concrete-slab building
in Friedrichshain

Performance di Vertical
Dance lungo la facciata di
un cosiddetto Plattenbau nel
quartiere di Friedrichshain

フリードリヒスハインの
鉄筋プレハブ住宅前で
のヴァーティカルダンス
のパーフォーマンス

23:45

Vor der
Gedächtniskirche

In front of the
Gedächtniskirche

Davanti alla
Gedächtniskirche

ゲデヒトニスキル
ヒェ教会前

Wintergarten Varieté

Variety show in the Wintergarten

Teatro di varietà Wintergarten

ヴィンターガルテン庭園
のヴァリエテ

Erik-Jan Ouwerkerk, geboren 1959 in Leiderdorp (Niederlande), studierte zunächst Biologie und wandte sich danach der Fotografie zu. Seit 1988 lebt er als freier Fotograf in Berlin. Im Nicolai Verlag sind mehrere Publikationen mit Fotografien von ihm erschienen, darunter die Bände »Neue Gartenkunst in Berlin« (2001) und »Berlin Sightseeing« (2002).

Erik-Jan Ouwerkerk, born in 1959 in Leiderdorp (Netherlands), studied biology before taking up photography. Since 1988 he has worked as a freelance photographer in Berlin. Nicolai has published several books with photos by Ouwerkerk, including "Neue Gartenkunst in Berlin" (New Garden Design in Berlin, 2001) and "Berlin Sightseeing" (2002).

Erik-Jan Ouwerkerk, nato a Leiderdorp (Olanda) nel 1959, ha studiato biologia per dedicarsi poi alla fotografia. Dal 1988 vive a Berlino, dove lavora come fotografo free-lance. La casa editrice Nicolai ha pubblicato vari volumi con sue fotografie, tra i quali e « Neue Gartenkunst in Berlin » (Nuova arte dei giardini a Berlino, 2001) e « Berlin Sightseeing » (2002).

エリク-ヤン・ウーヴァーカークは1959年にライダードープ（オランダ）に生まれた。生物を専攻した後写真に転向、1988年以来フリーの写真家としてベルリンに住む。ニコライ出版からは「新しいベルリンの庭園芸術」（2001）や「ベルリン観光」（2002）他、たくさんの作品が出版されている。

© 2004 Nicolaische Verlagsbuchhandlung GmbH, Berlin

© für Helmut-Newton-Foto (Bild zu 16.15 Uhr) bei der Newton Bar, Berlin

Übersetzungen: Miranda Robbins (Englisch)
Maria Cristina Francesconi (Italienisch)
Masami Ono-Feller (Japanisch)
Gestaltung: hawemannundmosch, Berlin
Satz u. Repro: Mega-Satz-Service, Berlin
Druck: Aumüller KG, Regensburg
Bindung: Kunst- und Verlagsbuchbinderei Leipzig

ISBN 3-89479-132-2